SPEAK!!!!!

God's Confessions for Me

NIKKI GEORGE

JT Publishing House

Speak It! God's Confessions for Me
Copyright © 2023 by Nikki George

Requests to the author for permission should be addressed to:
JT Publishing House, writing@jtpublishinghouse.com

Names: George, Nikki.
Title: Speak / Nikki George.
Description: Spartanburg: JT Publishing House, 2023. | Summary: "Speak It is a confessions book designed to create confidence while tackling low self-esteem or a poor self-image. Let your children intentionally speak the word of God over their lives and sow positive seeds for their future and those they encounter. The more they speak it, the more they will believe it.

Speak It: God's Confessions for Me aims to help develop happy and confident children everywhere. "-- Provided by publisher.
Identifiers: LCCN 2023937984 (print) | ISBN 9781954624153 (paperback) | ISBN 9781954624160 (ebook)
Subjects: BISAC: JUVENILE NONFICTION / Religious / Christian / Devotional & Prayer
LC record available at https://lccn.loc.gov/2023937984

Disclaimer: Any internet addresses (websites, blogs, etc.) and telephone numbers in this book are offered as a resource. They are not intended in any way to be or imply an endorsement by JT Publishing House or the author, nor does JT Publishing House vouch for the content of these sites and numbers for the life of this book.

Published by JT Publishing, Spartanburg, South Carolina
www.jtpublishinghouse.com

Printed in the United States of America
10 9 8 7 6 5 4 3 2 1

SPEAK IT!

God's Confessions for Me

Written by Nikki George

jt

publishing house

Dear Kids,

Once you know what God says about you, you have to agree with what He says and speak it! Keep reminding yourself (and sometimes others) what God says about you.

So many voices will try to tell you about yourself, but God created you and knows you're wonderful and powerful. He knows that you are created in His image and likeness.

God has some amazing plans for you, so keep seeing yourself as God sees you. You can Speak It! as you look in the mirror while you're getting dressed in the mornings. You can Speak It! over breakfast, and you can Speak It! before you go to bed at night.

Remember, God loves you, and there is power in your words, so don't keep all those good words locked up. Instead, let them out and Speak it!

I will write God's Word on my heart.
And give my life a great jumpstart.

"Let not mercy and truth forsake thee: bind them about thy neck; write them upon the table of thine heart:

So shalt thou find favor and good understanding in the sight of God and man.

Trust in the Lord with all thine heart; and lean not unto thine own understanding.

In all thy ways acknowledge Him, and He shall direct your paths."

~Proverbs 3:3-6

"I will give thanks and praise to You, for I
am fearfully and wonderfully made;

Wonderful are Your works,
And my soul knows it very well."

~Psalms 139: 14

I am fearfully and wonderfully made.
I have my God's DNA.

"What? know ye not that your body is the temple of the Holy Ghost which is in you, which ye have of God, and ye are not your own."

~1 Corinthians 6:19

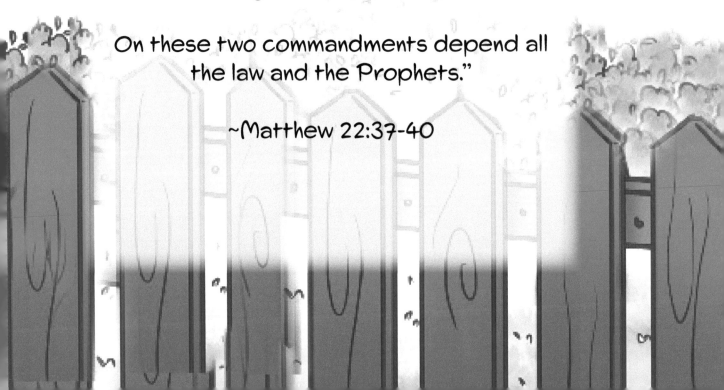

"You shall love the Lord your God with all your heart and with all your soul and with all your mind. This is the great and first commandment.

And a second is like it: you shall love your neighbor as yourself.

On these two commandments depend all the law and the Prophets."

~Matthew 22:37-40

I will love my neighbors, and I will love my God
with all my heart, soul, and mind.

"Apply your heart to instruction and your
ears to words of knowledge.
Give yourselves to disciplined instruction;
open your ears to tested knowledge."

~Proverbs 23:12

I will listen to and respect my teachers
I will be wise and encourage
God's people.

I will be kind to those in need
I will share what God has given me.

"Be kind to one another, tenderhearted, forgiving one another, as God in Christ forgave you."

~Ephesians 4:32

I will enjoy life and see good days.
I'll keep my confidence as I work and play.

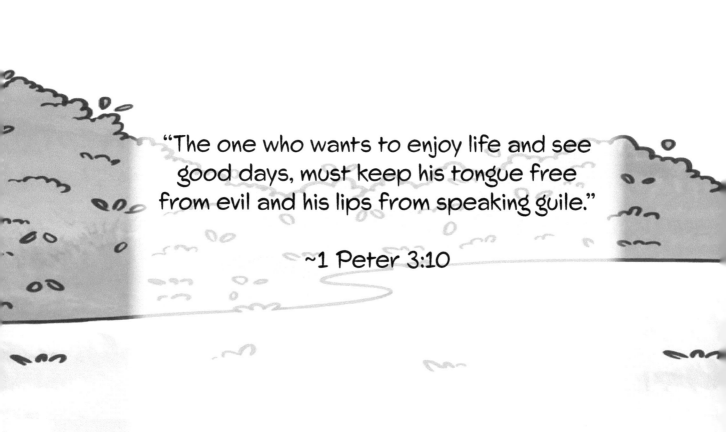

"The one who wants to enjoy life and see good days, must keep his tongue free from evil and his lips from speaking guile."

~1 Peter 3:10

I will be like an olive plant around the table.
Learning and sharing, a growing creative.

Your children will be like olive plants around your table.

~Psalms 128:3

I will lay down, and sleep in peace: for the LORD my God watches over me!

I will both lay me down, and sleep in peace: for thou, LORD, only makest me dwell in safety.

~Psalms 4:8

I Am God's Best

I am valuable
And worth great price
Because of the Blood of Jesus
And His awesome sacrifice.

I'll never see myself
Through the eyes of man
The One up above
Has a greater plan.

He has chosen me
From the foundation of time
I'm beautifully crafted,
Hand designed.

God made me special
I'm fearfully and wonderfully made
Before the womb, God knew me
The workmanship He would create.

I'm so unique
I have my own set of prints
I'm unlike any other
I show up and represent!

Author's Note

Parents,

Speak It! takes a handful out of the vast volumes of scriptures created to positively impact your child's life. The words of this book are designed to promote healthy self-esteem and confidence in children.

Words are powerful and hold the power within to create life or death. God spoke, and the world came to life. The world came into existence; it came into being.

God has created us in His image and after His likeness. He created us to be speaking beings. With this power, you can help guide your child into framing their world by creating the best outlook on life as they speak a fulfilling existence for themselves and their future.

God's words are seeds, and as they are spoken, they can be planted into your child's life as you watch them come to life and grow.

With so much negativity in the world, it's time to speak encouraging and positive words. It's time to speak hope and destiny, and it's time to speak life into the future generation.

As your child learns what the scriptures say about important topics such as love, identity, community, learning, and being respectful, they will internalize these wholesome values. They will have what they say as they confess God's words when they pray and Speak It!

Author's Bio

Nikki George is the author of Secret Place Poems and One God, One Message, One Day. She has actively served in children's ministry for years and loves to help the younger generation develop their identity in Christ. George streams and hosts The "i" Witness Show with Nikki George. She is also the owner of NikkiNovelties and Write Company Publishing.

The University of North Carolina at Charlotte Alumna is also an ordained Minister and has been blessed to have 28 years of marriage. She and her husband Maurice are the parents of seven children and have two grandchildren.

Nikki's mission is to help turn the hearts of the children back to the Father and be a witness that spreads the gospel of Jesus Christ throughout the world.

Printed in the USA
CPSIA information can be obtained
at www.ICGtesting.com
LVHW062221190124
769097LV00002B/50